Out in Space

A Can-You-Find-It Book

PEBBLE
a capstone imprint

Blast Off!

Can you find
these things?

crayon

bananas

fish

teddy
bear

snail

soda
can

tugboat

bluebird

whale

butterfly

Galaxy Delights

Can you find these things?

 globe

 hose

 lighthouse

 mermaid

| mask and snorkel | lamb | bird | gnome | poodle | tennis racquet |

Robot Fun Run

Can you find these things?

cheese

umbrella

iron

bow

spray bottle

fork

hot dog

bee

wizard hat

pencil

Walking on the Moon

Can you find these things?

sea horse

gumball machine

pitcher

trumpet

 birdcage

 mouse

 strawberry

 crown

 pretzel

 apple

Make a Wish!

Can you find
these things?

baseball

jet

polar
bear

elephant

daisy

toilet
paper

dragon

dust
pan

robot

bride

Big Star, Little Stars

Can you find these things?

 Saturn

 avocado

 taco

 koala

tissue
box

school
bus

pear

xylophone

deer

cupid

An Alien Welcome

Can you find
these things?

guitar

candle

watering
can

Pegasus

 heart

 starfish

 mushroom

 tulip

 olive

ice-cream cone

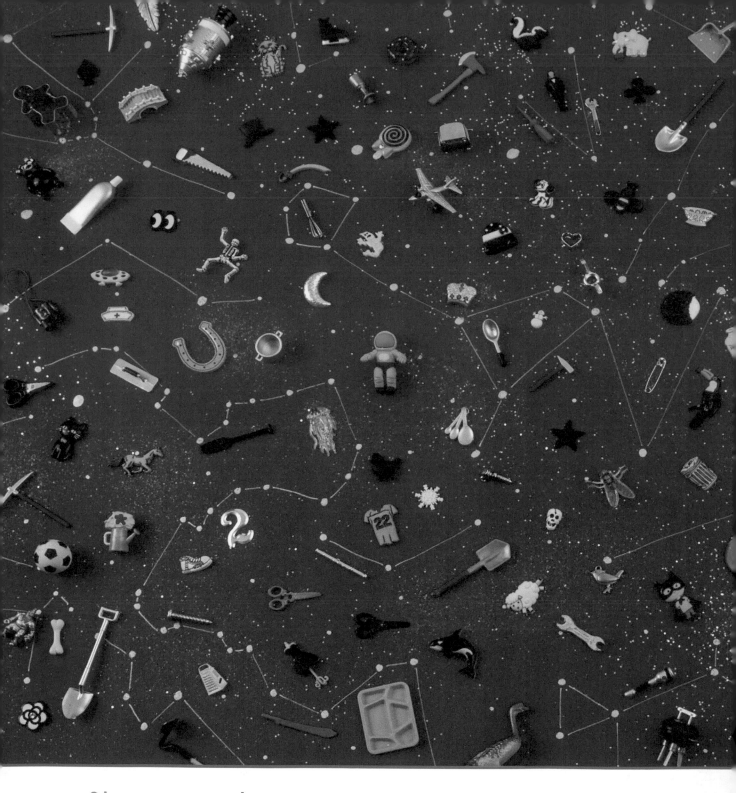

Star Pictures

Can you find these things?

ship

zebra

piano

soccer ball

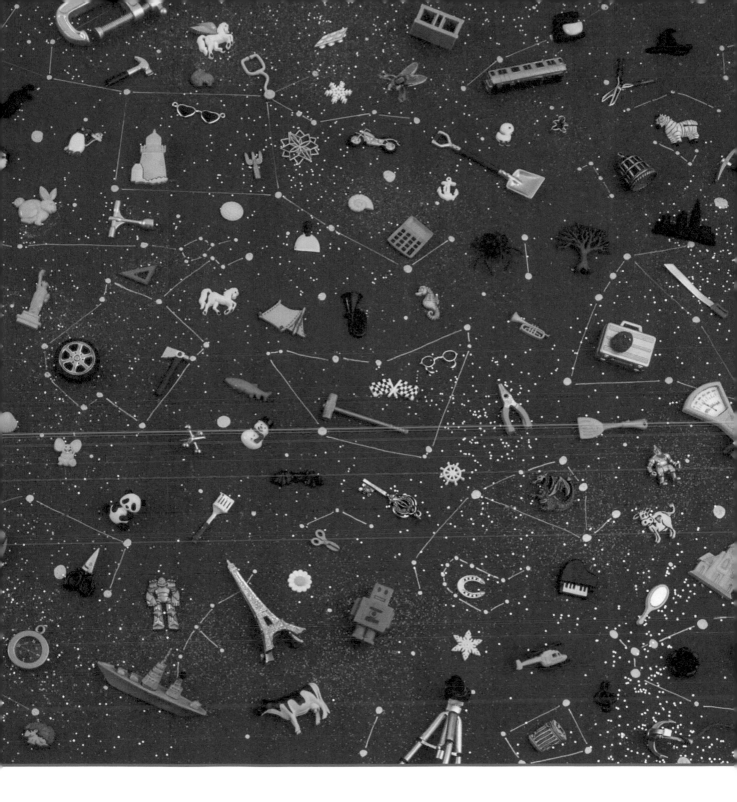

tent

ice
skate

killer
whale

saw

motorcycle

skull

So Many Satellites!

Can you find these things?

toucan

lion

horse

seal

hat

mitten

saxophone

scissors

owl

police car

Playful
Planets

Can you find
these things?

ant

dolphin

hot-air
balloon

comb

astronaut

ladybug

alien

sunflower

plum

witch's shoe

Looking at the Sky

Can you find these things?

egg

rose

yarn

fire hydrant

 doghouse

 purse

 lobster

 dragonfly

 cap

cactus

Marvelous Mars

Can you find
these things?

tiger

bike

corn

raccoon

anchor

jack-o'-
lantern

chef's
hat

fish
bones

snowman

spider

Lunar Eclipse

Can you find these things?

sewing machine

record

horseshoe

grill

 peach

 TV

 eagle

 clothespin

 billiard ball

 mixer

Space Camp

Can you find
these things?

fishbowl

ghost

golf
ball

cake

bunny   brush   llama   bowling pin   nurse   cowboy

Psst! Did you know that Pebs the Pebble was hiding in EVERY PUZZLE in this book?

It's true! Go back and look!

Look for other books in this series:

I would like to dedicate this book to my amazing and supportive family and friends—with a very special thank you to Heidi Thompson, my boss and my friend. Never thought that work could be so much fun. — KD

Pebble Sprout is published by Pebble, an imprint of Capstone.
1710 Roe Crest Drive, North Mankato, Minnesota 56003
www.capstonepub.com

Library of Congress Cataloging-in-Publication Data

Names: Dubke, Karon, author.
Title: Out in space : a can-you-find-it book / Karon Dubke.
Description: North Mankato : Capstone Press, [2021] | Series: Can you find it? | Audience: Ages 6-8 | Audience: Grades K-1 | Summary: "Send kids on an out-of-this-world seek-and-find adventure. Planets, moons, shooting stars, and countless other celestial objects make finding the hidden items in the full-color photo puzzles a blast. Pictographs and word labels are included in each to-find list"— Provided by publisher.
Identifiers: LCCN 2020030970 (print) | LCCN 2020030971 (ebook) | ISBN 9781977132130 (hardcover) | ISBN 9781977133151 (paperback) | ISBN 9781977154712 (ebook)
Subjects: LCSH: Outer space—Juvenile literature. | Outer space—Exploration—Juvenile literature.
Classification: LCC QB500.22 .D83 2021 (print) | LCC QB500.22 (ebook) | DDC 523—dc23
LC record available at https://lccn.loc.gov/2020030970
LC ebook record available at https://lccn.loc.gov/2020030971

Image Credits: All photos by Capstone Studio/Karon Dubke

Editorial Credits: Jill Kalz, editor; Heidi Thompson, designer; Karon Dubke, set stylist; Kathy McColley, production specialist